EASY
Money

CREATING WEALTH DOES NOT
NEED TO BE COMPLICATED

Written by

JENNIFER BENNETT, CPA

ISBN-13: 978-1546871897

For Dan, Zach, and Alex,
my love, my light, and my joy

CONTENTS

Why This Book?

This book is unlike any other personal-finance book on the market. Take one look inside, and you will see the difference. On each page is a key concept. If you get it, simply move on. If not, look on the other side of the page for a detailed explanation. You can read the entire book in just a few hours. Think Twitter meets personal finance.

But don't be fooled by the simple format. These are complex ideas presented in a manner that is not only easy to understand but also easy to implement in your life. It is not a get-rich-quick book. It is a get-the-most-out-of-your-money-so-you-can-get-the-most-out-of-life book. It gives ordinary people without trust funds and lottery winnings a way to create extraordinary wealth. And that makes all the difference. The concepts outlined, if applied, are transformative. That may sound a bit dramatic, but it is true. I have lived it.

And you can too.

Introduction

Remember, you can earn more money, but when time is spent, it is gone forever.

—Zig Ziglar

The single biggest and

easiest thing you can do to

build wealth is to save and

invest early.

Creating wealth boils down to a math problem involving time, money, and rate of return, otherwise known as compound interest. Compound interest is a very cool thing. Einstein even referred to it as the eighth wonder of the world. It provides a way for ordinary people without trust funds or lottery winnings to become financially free simply by starting early and investing over time.

Here is how it works. Assume you invest $1,000 at 10 percent. At the end of one year, you will have $1,100. If you reinvest the entire amount, at the end of the second year, you will have $1,210. Notice that in the second year, you earn $110 compared to the $100 you earn in the first year. You earn interest on your interest. By year ten, your investment will have grown to $2,593, and by year twenty your investment will be worth $6,727. Notice that in the first ten years, the investment grows by $1,593, but in the second ten years it grows by $4,134. Over time the compounding effect results in exponential growth.

If Sam, an eighteen-year-old, invested $500 a year a until age twenty-four and then invested $2,500 a year at 10 percent until age thirty, for a total investment of $20,500, at age sixty-five he would have $965,000.

If he waited until age twenty-eight to invest the same amount at the same rate, he would have $372,000.

Think about that for a minute. The only difference between having $965,000 and having $372,000 is *time*. Sam invests the same amount of money at the same rate of return. That is the power of compound interest.

The fact is that very few young people will take advantage of the time they have. Most squander that key advantage because they believe they must earn more, be a little more financially comfortable, or start their "career" jobs before beginning to save seriously. That is the traditional way of managing money, not the easy way.

Be the exception. It does not take much.

The second biggest thing you

can do to accumulate wealth

is to invest as much as you

can.

Remember, building wealth is a math problem (and who doesn't *love* math?). You saw how maximizing time dramatically affects your outcome. Maximizing the amount invested will have the same effect.

If Sam invested the same

$500 a year from age

eighteen to twenty-four and

then invested $5,000 a year

from age twenty-five to thirty

at the same 10 percent rate,

he would have

$1,698,000!

First, notice that I did not adjust the amount that Sam invested until age twenty-five based on assumptions about college and "real" jobs. Sam's total investment increased from $20,500 to $38,000. However, his account went from $965,000 to $1,698,000. That is the compounding effect of both time and money. Pretty cool, right?

(Just for kicks and giggles, if Sam could invest $5,000 a year from, let's say, age twenty to age thirty, he could retire with a portfolio of $2.6 million.)

The third biggest thing you can do to build wealth is to maximize your rate of return.

Rate of return is the amount you receive in return for investing in stocks, bonds, real estate, businesses, and other opportunities. I will cover the types of investments later in this book.

Based on the previous example, if Sam could earn 12 percent instead of 10 percent, he would have a mind-blowing $3,500,000!

I am sure you can see the trend here. Maximize one or all the components of compound interest, and you will be rich! The rest of this book is designed to teach you the easiest way to get there.

So why doesn't

everyone

save early and

live a life of wealth?

There are many reasons why people do not take advantage of compound interest. Few people really grasp the power of compounding. Our educational system and society focuses on earning our way to wealth. We are told from a young age to go to college and get a great-paying job, and the rest will take care of itself. Unfortunately, that simply is not true. You cannot earn our way to wealth. Earning without investing will never create wealth. And we are never told that investing even small amounts at a young age will transform the direction of our lives.

Second, investing means giving up something today for tomorrow. I've found that only people who have experienced true financial hardship are motivated to do what it takes to create wealth. The trick is to know that by saving and investing early, you are creating a different life today. It is not all about some future retirement date. It is about being in control along the way.

Finally, investments do not move in a straight line. Investments go up, go down, and stay flat. It is not pretty. Many people lose faith and allow fear or greed to take over, and as a result they make poor decisions. Here you will learn how money behaves and how you can take advantage of it.

Chapter One: Easy Money Mind-Set

Most anything I've ever set my mind to, I could accomplish.

—Kelly Slater

Decide to adopt the

Easy Money mind-set.

Decide, v.

To select a course of action.

Decide is a verb. Deciding to adopt the Easy Money mind-set, a process of becoming financially awake, creates focus and purpose. It changes creating wealth from a wish to a goal. Your thoughts immediately move from a dreamy, wishful state to a new, single-minded money consciousness. All your future financial decisions will be affected by your choice.

Get

organized.

To prove how organization affects your wallet, I want you to pick one area of your living space, such as a closet, your vanity, or the refrigerator. Take out everything. Make a list of everything that you bought and never used. Next list all the duplicate items. For instance, do you have five black shirts or four tubes of mascara? What did you find that you thought was lost? Add that to the list. Next add any actual money you found—maybe in a pocket, at the bottom of a purse, or tucked away in a drawer. Once you have completed the list, put a value next to each item, and total it up. This amount represents wasted money; more importantly, it represents wasted opportunity.

Here are some Easy Money organization tips:

1. Make daily to-do and to-buy lists.
2. Give everything a home.
3. Practice the one-touch rule. The one-touch rule involves fully completing a task the first time you "touch" it. Instead of rinsing a dish and putting it in the sink, rinse it and put it in the dishwasher.
4. Edit regularly.

Become

financially aware.

The first step toward financial freedom is really being aware of how you currently spend money. It is the small, mindless purchases that cause the most damage. For example, you buy a cup of coffee at the McDonald's drive-through for only $1.29 plus tax. You congratulate yourself for not spending $3.50 a cup like all your Starbucks-loving friends. No big deal, right? But here is the thing: although a dollar here or five dollars there does not seem like much per transaction, it adds up to big money at the end of each month—potentially life-changing money. Remember, Sam started by saving only $500 per year.

Start tracking your money to become financially aware. Consider using Mint (www.mint.com). Within minutes you can link your bank account to the app. If you make cash purchases, ask for a receipt for *all* transactions. At the end of the day, empty your wallet or purse into a receipt box. Do this for a minimum of a week, preferably for a month, and then look. My guess is that you will be really surprised.

Consciously change how you feel about spending money.

Over the long term, you will not stick with a plan that does not feel good. Make saying "no" to a purchase feel good. It is just a mind shift. It is not about lack or deprivation; it is all about getting control of your life. Savor that feeling of empowerment. If you find it hard in the beginning, avoid temptation. Leave credit cards at home. Instead of going to the mall, go to the park. Avoid the shopping channels and catalogs. Replace old spending habits with new ones. Celebrate each success.

A side note: Over the past five years, I have driven regularly past a trash dump and have watched it grow from a hill to a mountain. The sheer volume of trash is alarming. It has made me rethink my purchases on a whole new level. If you are looking for motivation beyond fattening your wallet and getting control of your finances, you can add being environmentally aware to your list of feel-good reasons for controlling your spending.

Make paying yourself first nonnegotiable.

This is the most important thing you need to get from this book. Most people develop a budget, look at how much they earn versus what they spend, and then develop some sort of savings goal. That is completely backward.

The Easy Money mind-set requires that you create your savings goal *first*. Set that money aside *first*. Then figure out how to live off the rest. This idea is fundamental to your success.

The federal government knows the importance of being paid first. That is why taxes are withheld from our paychecks; they know they would never see the money otherwise. Do you miss the taxes taken out of your paycheck? Likely not, because that money was never really available to spend in the first place. Your savings need to be given the same level of priority. Once you have paid yourself, who cares what you do with the rest?

You cannot earn your way to financial freedom.

Many people believe you earn your way to wealth. I once believed it too. But that is only half the equation. Earnings alone do not create wealth. In fact, according to a 2009 Sports Illustrated study, 78 percent of former NFL players are broke within two years of retirement. Vin Baker, an NBA player who earned over $100 million in his career, recently accepted a job as a manager at a Starbucks. These stories are not limited to athletes. There are plenty of once-high-earning inventors, actors, and musicians who are now bankrupt. How is that possible? Clearly what matters is not how much you earn but what you do with that money

Practice gratitude.

As you move through this process, you will no doubt encounter people who have more, spend more, and appear to be having the time of their lives. It is easy to get a little bitter, especially if you spend too much time on social media or watching reality television, such as *Keeping Up with the Kardashians*. But before you let yourself get hung up on what others have, you should really look at the millions who have less. There is a reason why people across the world desperately want to move to the United States. We are blessed simply because we were born in this country. It is a gift that should not be discounted.

The next time you are feeling sorry for yourself (it is natural from time to time) because things are hard (and they will be), count your blessings. Blessings are not about what you want but about what you already have. Blessings are things like friends, family, and pets, or facts such as that the sun is shining or that you live in a country of opportunity. It doesn't really matter what you count as a blessing. What matters is having a mind-set that cultivates optimism and happiness.

Chapter Two: Making Money

I am always doing that which I cannot do, in order that I may learn how to do it.

—Pablo Picasso

Your life and career are what you make of them.

There are no limitations.

I once watched a show about a young man in high school whose guidance counselor told a mother that her son would never amount to anything.

Can you imagine? Someone trained in helping young minds grow and see possibilities telling a young man's family there is no hope. That man quit high school. He is now reportedly worth over $50 million. His name is Allen Simon, and he is the inventor of the Wee Wee Pad, a puppy-housebreaking product.

What does that say to you? Was he the lucky one? Maybe. But I know landscapers who make solid six-figure annual salaries. I know hair stylists who make over $250,000 a year. I know CPAs who earn over $500,000 a year. I also know college graduates with math degrees who make less than $17,000 a year.

Life is what you make of it. Some people want a job without headaches; others want to conquer the world. It really doesn't matter how much money you make; it is what you do with that money that matters. Build a life of your choosing.

If you want to be the best,

do your best.

There are hugely successful companies built on this very premise. Two such companies are 1-800-GOT-JUNK? and College Hunks Hauling Junk. The founders of these companies are now multimillionaires. They were young men when they started these companies. Obviously, hauling junk does not require a special talent in and of itself. So why are these two companies prospering?

Many articles have been written about these companies and how they became so successful. Most of the articles focus on the expansion of the companies. But that success all started from a simple idea: Agree to do a job at an agreed-upon price. Show up on time, dressed neatly. Do a job that exceeds the customer's expectations at that agreed-upon price. Don't give up. Learn from your mistakes. Do it over and over again. Seems simple enough.

For many things in life, it is that little bit extra that makes a huge difference. In 212°: The Extra Degree, authors Sam Parker and Mac Anderson write: "At 211 degrees, water is hot. At 212 degrees, it boils. And with boiling water comes steam. And steam can power a locomotive." It is that extra degree of effort that transforms ordinary to extraordinary.

SAT scores have little power to predict earnings.

—JOHN CLOUD, "INSIDE THE NEW SAT," TIME MAGAZINE, OCTOBER 27, 2003

For too long, the educational system has made us believe that the only path to success is to do well in high school, kill your SATs, and get into a great college or university—then you are set. It is true there is a large disparity between the average lifetime earnings of people with college educations and those without. Furthermore, I believe education at all levels, formal and informal, helps society overall. But to imply that people will not be successful because they did not perform well on a standardized test or in college is just plain wrong.

You can no longer use the excuse "I am not smart enough to make more money." Didn't do well on the SAT? So, what? Larry Dean made a 750 on his SAT and earned over $30 million. Josey Parks, Myles Kovacs, and Brittany Pozzi are all millionaires who did not go to college. Success is about drive, perseverance, determination, and knowing whom to ask when you need help. Success is seeing things other people don't and doing things others won't.

Create a shortcut to success

by

seeking mentors and role

models.

Whether you are just starting out or have been working for a while, it is always a good idea to learn from people who have gone before you. They have already traveled the road you are on and can offer tips and ideas to make the road smoother. Some companies have formal mentoring programs; others do not. Either way, it is smart to align yourself with success, not in a spirit of "kissing ass" but in the spirit of learning the ropes.

If you don't have strong role models available, read. There are hundreds of biographies of successful people. Amid their stories are lessons that can be learned—ideas you might never have heard before. Their stories can also serve as a source of inspiration. Learn how they overcame obstacles, kept going when things looked tough, and turned apparent failure into success. No road to success is smooth and without delays. Otherwise the story would be really boring. You never know where your road might lead you.

What you think about,

you bring about.

"What you think about, you bring about" is a cliché that speaks to a fundamental truth. I would like to modify this statement by adding, "What you think about and believe about, you bring about." Your ability to succeed in any area of life depends more on what you believe about yourself than on what others believe. If you believe you are not worthy and cannot control your money or succeed in life, you will not succeed.

Emotional Intelligence, by Daniel Goleman, includes this statement by Albery Bandura, a Stanford psychologist who has done much research on self-efficacy: "People's beliefs about their abilities have a profound effect on those abilities. Ability is not a fixed property; there is a huge variability in how you perform. People who have a sense of self-efficacy bounce back from failure; they approach things in terms of how to handle them rather than worrying about what can go wrong."

Do yourself a favor: Take control of your thoughts. See yourself accomplishing your goals. Make such thoughts part of your mental landscape. Surround yourself with people who inspire you. Pay attention to the things that empower you. Be careful of television, movies, media, and even well-meaning relatives that will shift your focus. When "I can't" enters your mind, see it and discard it. Replace it with "I can and I will."

When seeking employment, experience matters.

The first job is always the hardest to find, because an employer wants experience, but how are you supposed to get experience unless you get the job? Ugh!

If you find yourself facing this dilemma, consider the following strategies:

1. Repackage your previous experiences to highlight skills needed in the new position. Were you a team captain? Did you organize a fund raiser? Did you hold a key position, such as president or treasurer of a club?

2. Look for an entry-level position to get your foot in the door.

3. Get special certifications. If you are an accountant, get your CPA license. Sharpen your business skills with free courses offered by Coursera.   A techie? Make sure that your skills are current. Look at free online coding courses offered by companies like MIT OpenCourseWare and Codecademy.

4. Network. Beginning today, create and maintain a LinkedIn account (LinkedIn.com). Ask for referrals; they are the best way to get a job.

5. Consider smaller companies; they are more likely to give someone a chance.

The highest paying job is

not always the

best choice.

When thinking about accepting a job offer, it is wise to think long term. Sometimes a lower-paying job is more in line with your long-term goals and ultimate career path. In that case, accepting a lower-paying job to gain experience in the field in which you plan to work is smart.

Also, when looking at multiple offers within the same field but in different locations, consider the cost of living. Making $45,000 in Nashville may net you more than making $60,000 in New York once you calculate rent, parking, taxes, and other costs.

Finally, when considering multiple employment opportunities, think about the culture and fit. This is important because you will be spending a significant amount of time with your fellow employees. If there is a fundamental disconnect, you will not be happy. An unhappy employee is not a productive employee. And an unproductive employee gets fired!

Consider a side hustle to make ends meet.

A side hustle can be anything that you can think of to make more money on the side. The Internet is full of ideas. Check out things like being an Uber driver, a tutor, a bookkeeper, a website designer, a coach, or a pet sitter. Here, too, by doing your best and exceeding expectations, you can make a nice bit of side money. By the way, 1-800-GOT-JUNK? started out as a side hustle to pay for college. Just saying.

Clean up

your social media.

Whether you own your own business or work for someone else, make sure your social media profiles fit the professional image you are trying to portray, even if all your settings are private. Simple enough.

Chapter Three: Managing the Money You Make

In reading the lives of great men, I found that the first victory they won was over themselves...self-discipline with all of them came first.

—Harry S. Truman

Calculate your

net worth.

This is a simple exercise. On one side of a piece of paper, list the market value of everything you own—what you could sell it for. On the other side of the paper, list everything you owe. Then subtract the debt (what you owe) from your assets (what you own). The result is your net worth.

The distinction between net worth and assets is critical. Anyone can look like a hotshot by living in a huge house and driving the latest, coolest sports car and still be one misstep away from being homeless. Those people are posers. They look like something they are not. Trust me: this happens more than you could ever imagine. True wealth is measured in what you get to keep after paying everyone back.

If you have a positive net worth or even zero net worth, that is a decent place to start. If, however, you are starting out in the negative, determine why. Do you have student loans? Not so bad, because the debt represents the promise of higher future earnings. On the other hand, if you are using credit to live beyond your means, you are playing a dangerous game that usually ends badly.

Calculate your cash flow
by subtracting your expenses
from income.

Begin by recording your income. This will be easy or difficult depending on the way you are paid. If you get paid the same amount every month, you are done. Write that number at the top of the page next to Income. On the other hand, if you are paid a weekly amount that includes tips or commissions, you will need to total several months to get an average.

Next, record all your expenses: Monthly recurring expenses such as rent, insurance, savings and phone; Non-monthly expenses like contact lenses refills, prescriptions, dental appointments, and discretionary expenses like clothing and entertainment. (Remember to convert non-monthly expenses to an average monthly expense.)

Analyze the results.

Scenario 1: Your income is greater than your expenses, and your checking/savings account balance is growing each month. Yeah! This is a great start!

Scenario 2: Your income is greater than your expenses, but your checking/savings account balance is not growing each month. Something is wrong. Go back and reevaluate your income and expenses. If you cannot identify the problem, start tracking your money from this point on.

Scenario 3: Your income is less than your expenses, but your checking/savings account balance is growing each month. This can occur for several reasons. One possibility is that, as in scenario 2, you have estimated your income or expenses incorrectly. Take another look. Another possibility is that your account is growing temporarily as you accumulate money for your nonmonthly expenses, but when they come due, you will be short. The third and most troubling possibility is that you are using debt and/or credit cards to get by. That is financially catastrophic and requires immediate action. Debt, especially credit card debt, will ruin you financially because it carries such high interest rates.

Scenario 4: Your income is less than your expenses, and your checking/savings account balance is not growing each month. In this scenario, you will run out of money. You need to either earn more or spend less. Just because it is easy doesn't mean it is fun.

Budgeting is like dieting: they work temporarily but to achieve lasting results you must change your habits.

At this point you should have a pretty clear picture of your net worth and past spending habits. (If not, go back and try again.) For many people, this process is like stepping on the scale and finding that they gained ten pounds without really knowing it and then pledging to go on a strict diet, now! The problem is that diets and budgets don't work, for one reason: they are short-term solutions to long-term behavior.

In addition, both strategies are geared toward what you can't do. Don't eat chocolate; don't spend more than fifty dollars at the salon. What happens to people who can't live without a little chocolate each day or who are really particular about their hair? Are they going to stick to a strict plan? Probably not.

Instead, start with making a nonnegotiable commitment to pay yourself first. Then structure a life that you consciously enjoy, and eliminate the financial clutter. In the beginning this will be harder to accomplish because so much of your earned income will go toward basic living expenses. Because of that, you need to be extra diligent and aggressively reduce or eliminate nonessential, "no enjoyment" expenditures. Start with the easy stuff. Look at your monthly subscription services, such as gym memberships, premium cable channels, and paid radio. Annually, do comparison shopping for your insurance. Splurge on the stuff that really makes you happy (after investing, of course).

Consider the true cost of your purchases.

When I was younger, I was a spender. If I had a nickel, I spent it. Primarily because I thought I had to earn my way to wealth, and I wasn't earning much, so what was the point of saving? That, of course, changed when I was introduced to the concept of the time value of money. Holy guacamole, I could become rich simply by saving! That was something I could do, and it forever changed the way I made purchasing decisions.

For example, I worked in downtown Orlando. As in all cities, parking in Orlando was expensive. Whenever possible, I parked for free and walked the six or more blocks to work. In 1990, parking was roughly $5 a day, or $1,200 a year. Based on the compounded return of the Dow Jones Industrial Average (DJIA) as of July 2015, that $1,200 I saved on parking and invested is worth roughly $14,233. Totally worth it.

I must admit that I do not approach all financial decisions this way. I have traveled to many wonderful and beautiful places. And I am sure that if I applied time-value-of-money calculations to all my travel expenses, the result would be astounding. But I can honestly say that the money I spent on travel was totally worth it. By prioritizing my purchases differently, I was able to make better decisions to enrich my life today and tomorrow, and you can too.

Use technology to

stay on track.

Tracking income, paying bills, and monitoring savings and investing goals each month is a chore. In the past, handling those chores manually was the only option, but not anymore. Today many if not all financial chores can be automated. Here are some of the tasks you should consider automating:

1.Have your paycheck automatically deposited.

2.Automatically transfer money from checking to savings for near-term expenditures, such as nonmonthly expenses, and to build up your emergency fund and save for other anticipated expenses, such as a wedding, dream vacation, or home down payment.

3.Schedule monthly transfers from your checking account to your investment account. Consider automatic investment platforms such as Wealthfront (Wealthfront.com) and Betterment (Betterment.com).

4.Set up automatic bill pay.

5.If you cannot pay a bill automatically, set a monthly reminder on your phone to alert you that the bill is due.

6.Set up account-balance alerts to notify you when your account balances fall below a preset amount.

There is no single more important skill required to achieve financial success than managing the money you make.

The ability to save and invest regardless of your income is critical to your success. Earning without investing means a lifetime of earning, a life without choice. There will always be a reason to put off saving. Something is on sale. Your friends invite you out. There is a game you simply can't miss. It really doesn't matter what the excuse is. What matters is that if you postpone saving or go back and dip into your savings, you are not getting ahead. You are getting stuck.

If you are having trouble, know that getting control of your money is a learned skill that will improve over time. But don't take too long, because the cost of procrastinating is severe. To guarantee success, eliminate all temptation. Automate your savings and investing. Have the money taken out of your earnings or bank account before you ever see it. Second, keep your investments out of reach in a tax-deferred account such as a 401(k) or an individual retirement account (IRA). And finally, under no circumstances get into short-term debt.

Chapter Four: Creating Goals

Planning is bringing the future into the present so that you can do something about it now.

—Alan Lakein

You can't teach hungry.

—JOHN MORGAN

Motivation is at the very heart of success. You must want it, hunger for it. Goals are about quantifying what exactly it is that you want. As you think about your goals, tap into that desire. What is it you really hunger for and will be truly motivated to achieve?

Create goals based on things that you can control.

The difference between a wish and a goal is the ability to achieve the desired outcome. I am all in favor of wishes and daydreams. I certainly have dreams beyond my current ability to achieve them. I live that alternate reality on Pinterest, where I plan my dream house, go on exotic vacations, and have a closet beyond compare. It is fun, but it doesn't provide a clear path for translating dreams into reality.

Having goals such as "I will increase my sales by 15 percent," "I will get a 10 percent raise this year," or "My investments will grow by $7,500 by the end of this year" may seem empowering, but they are in fact wishes. They are not within your absolute control to achieve.

Instead, create actionable plans that are entirely within your control to accomplish. Here are some examples of definable plans:

•"I will make five additional sales calls each month."

•"I will complete the online computer programming course by April of next year to increase my earning potential."

•"I will save $500 a month."

Notice the difference? These goals are based on action as opposed to outcome.

Set specific

feel-good goals.

To make a lasting change in your life, you must anticipate a payoff. Writing down your goals quantifies the payoff you expect to receive. For a goal to be effective, it must be measurable, attainable, and time sensitive. Furthermore, a goal should be stated in terms of the outcome you want, not the outcome you are avoiding. This wording keeps your focus on the positive outcome.

Let's look at an example. Mary wants to save $20 a week. Her goal could be either

•"I will stop spending money on going out to lunch and save twenty dollars a week."

or

•"I will save $20 a week, for a total of $1,040 a year."

Both goals call for saving twenty dollars a week. But the first goal is written in terms of what she should give up. Fail. It feels like a sacrifice. The second goal requires that she save twenty dollars regardless of where the money comes from.

Based on the first goal, if Mary goes to lunch with her coworkers, she has failed. Fail long enough, and you quit. But using the second goal, she would simply rethink the week and find the twenty dollars somewhere else.

I know this sounds like psychobabble, but the fact is that we will not do something long term that is painful. Develop specific positive goals and actions. Make your goals feel good.

Commit to the three must-have financial goals.

We are all unique individuals. Our financial goals are our own. However, I define the following three objectives as musts for everyone.

1. Keep a buffer in your checking account. Start with $1,000.

2. Establish an emergency funds for unemployment or underemployment. Plan on three to twelve months of living expenses depending on your personal circumstances and risk tolerance.

3. Invest for your future. Start with a minimum of five percent of your gross earnings and increase by one percent it every 6 months.

These are the very basics. Obviously, there are many more goals, such as buying a home, traveling around the world, paying for college for your (eventual) children, having the ability to give back in a meaningful way, buying a vacation home, or owning your own business. Yet these three basics hold true regardless of your other personal financial ambitions.

Prioritize.

If you are just starting out, you may be wondering where to begin. Start with having a buffer in your checking account for everyday emergencies. Second, if you have outstanding balances on credit cards with high interest rates, pay them off. Credit card debt is toxic to your financial health. (More about that later.)

Next, balance investing between establishing your emergency fund and building long-term savings. This goes directly against what most advisors recommend. Most advisors recommend fully funding your emergency fund before adding to your long-term investments. But unless you have serious excess cash, you should balance your objectives between the two. To forgo long-term investing in favor of a healthy emergency fund will cost you more in the long run. It takes away the biggest advantage you have: time. The best solution is to keep living expenses at a minimum, especially when starting your career. Think college-level living that allows you to contribute toward your long-term goals and still cover your living expenses with almost any job if things get rough.

Automate your savings because you can't spend what you don't see.

Today it is easier than ever to automate your savings even with small amounts. Simply set up a monthly transfer from your bank to one of the automatic investment platforms like Wealthfront (Wealthfront.com) or Betterment (Betterment.com). They will invest even small amounts in a diversified portfolio of low cost exchange traded funds and periodically rebalance the portfolio to keep you on track with goals and objectives. In the past, this level of service and diversification was only available to those with substantial investment portfolios.

This is a great thing! I wish it were available when I was first starting out. What I love most is that it is easy. Once you have set it up, it will run on auto pilot thereby eliminating temptation and procrastination! It supports a habit and financial habits are what ultimately dictate your financial future.

Chapter Five: Debt: A Four-Letter Word

Debt, n.

An ingenious substitute for the chain and whip of the slave driver.

—Ambrose Bierce, The Devil's Dictionary, 1911

Borrow money to pay for things that will increase in value.

If you borrow only to purchase things that will increase in value over time while you repay the debt, your net worth will grow. After all, that is the whole point.

Given this rule, you may borrow to purchase a home (assuming you do not overpay for it), make an investment (more about this later), and pay for an education (assuming the degree or extra education will pay you back plus some in terms of extra earning potential). You may not borrow to pay for furniture, electronics, and vacations.

There is an exception to this rule, and that is related to purchasing a car. For most areas in the United States, you will need a car to get to and from work. You need the money from work to pay for the car. What comes first, the chicken or the egg? In this case, it is OK to borrow for a car. But that doesn't mean running off to the new-car lot and signing up for five to six years of payments, even if the interest rate is lower. Finance a reliable used car, go to work, and pay off the loan like crazy.

It's NEVER a good idea to carry balances on credit cards.

Credit cards, in and of themselves, are not a bad thing. It is when they are used to finance a lifestyle you could not otherwise afford that they are a bad thing—a really bad thing.

So how do you know whether you are using credit to live beyond your means? Do you have an outstanding balance? If the answer is yes, you are living beyond your means. It is really that simple.

Companies spend millions to get you hooked on credit. They offer free airline tickets, special cardholder discounts, and other incentives. The sneakiest strategy is deferred financing—no payments and no interest for ninety days, six months, or even a year. It really doesn't matter. What does matter is that when the balance comes due and you don't have the money to pay off the entire amount, guess what—that free financing is suddenly not so free. You owe interest from the original purchase date!

If you are disciplined, you can use the credit cards to take advantage of promotions and discounts, as long as you pay off the entire balance.

Credit cards work harder

against you than your

investments will work for you.

Just for kicks and giggles, let's pretend that you have $10,000 in credit card debt at 18 percent interest (not the highest allowed, by the way) and $10,000 in investments earning 8 percent. Your net worth is zero, even though you have $10,000. Let's also pretend that you have $250 a month that you can use either to pay down your credit card or to invest.

Scenario 1: You put the full $250 toward your debt each month and leave your investment alone. After five years, your net worth will have gone from zero to $14,898. You are moving in the right direction, but $250 a month for five years equals $15,000.

Scenario 2: On day 1, you liquidate your investment and pay off your credit card. Then you invest $250 a month, earning the same 8 percent. After five years, your net worth will be $18,369.

In both cases, you saved $250 a month. The only difference is what you did at the beginning. That is a $3,471 decision. Easy Money. If you are paying more in interest than you are earning on your investments, pay off your credit cards.

It is always a good idea to have an excellent credit rating.

A credit score, also known as your FICO score, is simply a number that banks and lenders use to determine whether they will lend you money and at what interest rate. The better the score, the lower the interest rate.

Generally speaking, the breakdown is as follows:

760–850   You get an A+.

700–759   Still great but not the top of the class.

680–699   Very good.

660–679   Normal/average range.

640–659   Needs some improvement.

Below 640 What the hell happened?

Review your credit report and FICO score.

There is a difference between your credit report and your FICO score. Your credit report is a summary of credit transactions. It is a list of available credit, outstanding balances, and total credit available. This information is used to calculate your FICO score. If the information on your credit report is inaccurate, your FICO score will also be inaccurate. A FICO score is what lenders use to determine whether you are creditworthy. Your FICO score is calculated by three different companies: Equifax, Experian, and Transunion. The scores can vary slightly.

You can receive a free credit report each year. It is a good idea to review your report each year to make sure that everything is correct. Go to AnnualReport.com to get your truly free report. It is quick and easy. Unfortunately, you must be a little more careful trying to get your FICO score. Otherwise you could end up paying a monthly credit-monitoring subscription fee. If you plan to use a free service, expect to be solicited—that is how they make money. (Nothing is really free.)

There is more to your credit rating than just paying on time.

Several things go into determining your FICO score. Your credit score is made of the following:

Payment history 35%

Amount owed   30%

Length of payment history   15%

New credit 10%

Types of credit   10%

Obviously, paying on time has a big impact on your score. But other things account for the remaining 65 percent. The amount-owed portion is the amount owed versus the credit limit. The credit bureaus do not like it if you have borrowed up to your maximums. I get that, but sometimes it can get a little weird.

For example, when I was refinancing my home, I closed out some old outstanding credit cards I had opened only to get the discounts. Because I'd closed the accounts, my ratio of outstanding credit to credit available increased. If I'd had a significant amount of available credit, that move could have seriously hurt my credit rating. Go figure.

Next comes the length of your credit history. A longer history gives lenders a better picture of your long-term habits.

The remaining 20 percent is the amount of new credit and the types of credit. If there is a significant amount of new credit, it makes creditors think that something is up. Also, they prefer to see different types of credit, such as credit cards, auto loans, and mortgages.

You don't have to be in debt to have an excellent credit rating.

Remember that your credit rating is made up of other things besides just paying on time. The credit rating agencies like to see different types of credit and a low ratio of outstanding balance to available credit. The trick is to get different types of credit without actually carrying a balance. It is not as hard as you think.

Let's say you go to a department store intending to buy a washer and dryer. You have the money saved. The store offers you 10 percent off the total purchase if you open a store credit card. Now, they are hoping you will open the account, spend your saved cash on something else, and pay them 22 percent compounded annually—a sweet deal for the department store.

To make this a sweet deal for you, open the account and save the 10 percent on the purchase. When the bill arrives, pay it in full. If they try to confuse the deal by offering both 10 percent savings and deferred financing, still pay it off right away. You have done several things: you have established credit, paid the balance, and gotten a discount to boot.

A good credit rating will save you thousands over your lifetime.

Consider this. Below is a table from the loan savings calculator at MyFICO.com. It provides average mortgage rates by FICO score, as of August 2015. The payments are based on a thirty-year loan for $250,000. A borrower with a high credit score will pay $84,711 less than a borrower with a poor FICO score. Same loan but $84,711 less. Easy Money!

Your FICO score	Your interest rate (%)	Your monthly payment ($)	Total payments over life of loan ($)
760–850	3.66	1,145	412,272
700–759	3.88	1,177	423,625
680–699	4.06	1,202	432,792
660–679	4.27	1,233	442,011
640–659	4.70	1,297	466,990
620–639	5.25	1,381	496,983

A home mortgage is not the only thing affected by your credit rating. Utility companies and insurance companies also take a look. A good credit rating can mean the difference between having to put down a substantial security deposit and having that money working for you.

If you have not established credit, start small.

If you are without a credit history, apply for a credit card. Go to BankRate.com and look for a card with no fees. Apply for that card. You can also consider secured credit cards and a cosigner. If you get approved, charge a small purchase each month, and pay off the balance. The easiest way to make regular purchases is to have a recurring bill, such as a phone bill or an insurance premium, paid automatically with the card. Then have the credit card payment automatically withdrawn from your checking account. You must pay the bills either way; you may as well build a good credit rating along the way. Easy Money.

After six months to a year, ask for an increase in the credit limit. Over time, build your credit profile by applying for additional credit. Please understand: I am not suggesting that you finance a purchase. Simply charge a normal purchase and pay off the bill.

ALWAYS

pay on time.

Let me give you a real-life example. Somebody—we will call him Joe—made a $165.00 purchase on a credit card. The bill came due. The minimum payment was $22.00. Instead of paying the entire balance, he made the minimum payment. In addition, he made the minimum payment one day late. The next month, he charged an additional $586.00 on that card.

Guess what happened. His next bill included a $39.00 penalty for the late payment and $9.75 in interest charges. That $22.00 minimum payment did nothing. With the late-payment penalty and the interest charge, he essentially threw away $50.00.

I am not making this up. I saw the statement from the credit card company. One misstep and they will hammer you. That is not Easy Money. Pay the bill on time, every time. That is Easy Money.

Establishing credit is not about establishing a lifestyle.

Temptation surrounds us. We are a consumer driven society. The last thing you want to do is to derail your financial goals by a trip to the mall. Make it easy on yourself; leave your credit card at home. Establishing credit is not meant to create a lifestyle. It is just a tool to save money on big future purchases, such as a home—nothing more.

If you are already in over your head, pay off your credit cards before all else.

Start today.

If you are already in over your head with credit card debt, you are not alone. This is not the time to feel bad, guilty, or ashamed. Those feelings will paralyze you or cause you to stick your head in the sand. Millions of people are in over their heads. It is a nationwide epidemic. Resolve this today: that is no longer your path. It is crash-diet time. Make it a priority to pay off those cards before all else.

There is no easy way to do this. It is not fun. But the result is worth the effort. Cut all nonessential spending. This requires a radical change in behavior—today. Time is of the essence. Remember the examples of compounding interest at the beginning. Compound interest works equally for you and against you. It does not discriminate. Every day, those cards are adding interest, adding debt. Day in and day out. Not only are they adding to your debt load, they are preventing you from adding to your investments.

Do whatever it takes to get rid of the debt. Celebrate your victories as you watch your balances decrease. Know that you are strong and in control of your life and future. Keep those feelings in mind if you get tempted to step off the path toward financial freedom.

Create a get-out-of-debt action plan.

Review your current spending plan and determine how much you are going to dedicate toward your debt. Next make a list of all your credit cards, store cards, and any other revolving short-term debt. For each debt, list the name, amount owed, interest rate, and minimum payment. Add the minimum payments, and subtract the total from the amount you have budgeted to pay off debt. That remainder is the extra amount you are going to pay on your targeted pay-off card.

Now select a card to pay off. If you have one or two small cards that can be paid off quickly, pay them off first. That will eliminate the clutter and keep you focused. Otherwise, focus on the card with the highest interest rate. Consider keeping track of the balances in Mint or Quicken. As you eliminate a card, add the minimum payment amount to the next targeted card. Repeat until all the cards are paid in full.

Celebrate each success along the way.

Chapter Six:
Easy
Economics

Economy is the basis of society. When the economy is stable, society develops.

—Morihei Ueshiba

Economics, n.

The science that deals with

the production, distribution,

and consumption of goods

and services, or the material

welfare of humankind.

Oh yeah, that explains it. You are not alone if you are confused by the definition of economics. Universities across the United States are equally split on whether the study of economics is a liberal art, a science, or part of the business school, probably because it is a little of each.

Economics is part math and part psychology. Gross domestic product (GDP), the value of all goods and services produced over a specified time period, is used to measure the economy. The inflation-adjusted change in GDP from one period to the next measures economic growth. That is the math part.

Yet the economy is much more than the sum of all sales. It reflects how we feel about our future. That is the psychology part. When we as a group feel good and are confident about the future, we spend money. When we spend, businesses earn greater profit. They in turn hire more employees and invest in further expanding their business. Unemployment falls and business investment increases. The nightly news says, "All is good," so we spend even more. GDP increases and an economic expansion is under way.

On the other hand, when we as a country are not confident about the future, we limit spending on the "extras." Businesses earn less profit, limit capital investment, and lay off some employees. The nightly news programs report an increase in the unemployment rate and lower GDP growth. People get a little more nervous, spend even less, and the entire cycle begins in the opposite direction.

The economy is made up of markets.

On a global level, an economy is made up of a web of transactions between buyers and sellers. Each thread of the web represents a market. There is a market for eggs, sugar, oil, labor, homes, stocks, bonds, and all other products and services. Within each market, there are buyers and sellers, all of whom are acting in their own best interests. The sellers are trying to maximize the price, and the buyers are trying to minimize the price.

Markets are affected by the forces of supply and demand.

Supply refers to the availability of goods and services for sale; demand refers to the desire for those goods and services. Suppliers of goods and services aim to maximize price whereas, buyers want to minimize price. The market price of goods and services represents the balance between the supply and demand.

Many factors that influence supply and demand are outside the scope of this book. But what you need to understand is the impact of supply and demand on the financial markets particularly.

Here's a case in point. Over the last year, Apple stock has traded at between $92 and $134 per share, with a current value of $110. The number of shares available for sale did not change. So why the big price swing? The price swings are purely a function of supply and demand. On a given day, if there are more sellers than buyers, the price falls to attract sufficient buyers. Sellers leave the market when the price gets too low. If there are more buyers than sellers, the price increases. Buyers leave the market when the price gets too high. It is really that easy. At the end of the day, when you see that the Nasdaq, Dow, or S&P 500 increased (more about them later), you know there was more demand for stocks on that particular day. The hard part is figuring out why.

Demand is not always rational.

Did you know that people clamor to buy Birkin handbags for as much as $150,000? That is not a typo. Is the demand rational? Clearly not.

Irrational demand is not limited to consumer goods and services. It affects the financial markets as well. In 1996, Alan Greenspan, then the Federal Reserve Board chairman, gave a now-famous speech in which he asked whether investors have an "irrational exuberance" for stocks. The Nasdaq, a stock index comprising primarily technology-based stocks, had increased by 66 percent in the previous two years, from 776 on December 31, 1994, to 1,290 on December 31, 1996. Despite Greenspan's warning, these stocks continued to increase at unprecedented levels. On December 31, 1999, the Nasdaq closed at 4,069, and it reached a high of 5,058* on May 10, 2000. This later became known as the dot-com bubble.

But even schoolchildren know that bubbles pop, especially big ones. By October 9, 2002, the Nasdaq had fallen to 1,141. A bursting bubble has a ripple effect throughout the economy. Consider that economic growth is dependent on how we feel about our financial future. Watching our investments double and triple makes us feel good. We spend money. This phenomenon is commonly called the wealth effect. The economy grows. Watching investments disintegrate makes us feel bad. Really bad. So, we cut back. You know the rest of the story.

* Yahoo Finance, http://www.finance.yahoo.com. Index adjusted for stock splits and dividends.

Irrational markets are fueled by fear and greed.

Looking back, it easy to see that it was not a good idea to buy into the Nasdaq in 1999 or to sell in 2002. But that is exactly what people were doing. The index tells us so. In 1999, there was excess demand for stocks. Sellers were able to demand a premium for stocks. Buyers willing paid it. In 2002, the opposite was true. Sellers were forced to lower their price to entice buyers to invest in stocks. The question is, why would reasonable people, professional people, behave this way?

Extreme markets are fueled by fear and greed. When markets are exploding, greed sets in with the lure of some quick cash. Professional money managers are the worst offenders because they are paid on short-term performance. If they miss out, they might get fired. On the way down, it is fear that reigns supreme. Selling seems like the only way to keep at least what you have left.

In hindsight, it seems easy to identify out-of-control markets. But it is harder in real life. When your neighbor talks about how he just doubled his money in a stock or made thousands on a house flip, it can be difficult to avoid the temptation to follow his example. Alternatively, when you watch your investments melt before your eyes, it is easy to think, "I need to get out now!" The stress of missing out on the top and riding down to the bottom can be intense.

The key to success when encountering ridiculous markets is to "attempt to be fearful when others are greedy and to be greedy only when others are fearful," as Warren Buffett, arguably the most successful investor of our time, so aptly said.

Whenever things get a little scary, think regression to the mean.

Regression to the mean can also be called the law of averages. It helps me sleep at night. It means everything returns to the average. What goes up comes down, and what goes down comes up. This is extremely important to keep in mind during turbulent times.

Consider the extreme example of the Nasdaq. Looking back over the twenty years between December 1989 and December 2009, we see that the Nasdaq increased by an average of 13 percent per year. In 1998, the index increased by 39 percent, followed by an 85 percent increase in 1999. By May 10, 2000, the Nasdaq had reached an astounding high of 5,048! The network news channels and the personal-finance magazines were saying there was still more money to be made. "Buy, buy, buy" was their battle call. Everyone forgot about regression to the mean; it was party time.

Just six months later, however, the party was over. By December 28, 2000, the index had lost 50 percent. Those same guys who just a few months earlier had been telling people to buy when the index was at 5,000 were now telling people to sell, sell, sell. The index eventually bottomed out at 1,230. That is a 75 percent loss. Just a little math lesson: When you lose 75 percent, you must make to make 300 percent to break even.

Now, here is the trick. I am not saying to time the market. Far from it. But if you know the Nasdaq earns an average of 13 percent, you must know that when the market has shot up by 150 percent or fallen by 75 percent, change is coming.

Chapter Seven: Investments

Fortune favors
the prepared mind.

—Louis Pasteur

You do not need to be rich to invest, you need to invest to be rich!

Thinking you need to be rich before you begin investing is synonymous with saying, "Once I reach my goal weight, I will begin my diet." It makes no sense. The only way to create wealth, other than by inheriting it or winning it, is through investing. As discussed at the beginning of this book, even small amounts of money can make a substantial difference.

If you get nothing else out of this book, get this:

•Decide that creating personal wealth is important.

•Pay yourself first; live off the rest.

•Invest. If you are unsure where to start, use automated investment platforms like Wealthfront and Betterment.

There are eight types of investments.

Investments are anything to which you devote time and money with the expectation of receiving even greater money in the future. Below is a list of common and not-so-common investments:

1. Yourself. Investments that take the form of obtaining or improving job skills through apprenticeship or college. Investing in yourself can also mean opening a business. Most the millionaires discussed in The Millionaire Next Door, by Thomas J. Stanley, were successful entrepreneurs.

2. Cash. Money held in savings accounts, money market accounts, and certificates of deposit.

3. Bonds. Loans to local, state, and federal governments or to corporations.

4. Stocks. Investments that make you a partial owner of a corporation.

5. Real estate.

6. Currencies. Trades of currencies as they change in value relative to one another.

7. Commodities. Raw materials that can be bought and sold. Examples include gold, silver, copper, oil, wheat, and corn.

8. Collectibles. Items that are perceived to have value. Examples include art, certain cars, and baseball cards.

I will focus on investing in yourself, cash, bonds, stocks, and real estate. Currencies, commodities, and collectibles have a speculative component that is outside the scope of this book.

There is a direct relationship between risk and reward.

Risk is uncertainty. Reward is the expected outcome. The more uncertainty, the more potential income is demanded by rational investors. On one side of the spectrum are bank-insured savings accounts. There is a very high degree of certainty that the money you put into a savings account will still be there when you need it; therefore, this type of investment offers the lowest return.

On the other side of the spectrum are collectibles. In August 2014, a 1962 Ferrari 250 GTO sold at auction for a record-breaking $38 million. The Ferrari originally sold for $18,000, and its value went down to $2,500 in 1969. The value of the car was based solely on the buyer's perception. As with all markets, that value comes down to supply and demand. There are very few of these cars available, but there is no guarantee that in the future there will be some stupidly rich person willing to pay even more money for a car that is more than fifty years old. High uncertainty, high potential reward.

As an investor, you are either an owner who shares in profits or a lender who receives interest.

All eight types of investments can be broken down into two classifications: you are either an owner or a lender. As an owner, you expect to receive profit from your investment in the form of greater value and/or earnings. Ownership-type assets include privately held businesses, stocks, and real estate.

As a lender, you expect to receive your investment plus interest. You act as a lender when you have a savings account, a money market, or a certificate of deposit, or when you invest in treasuries, municipals, and corporate bonds. The difference between all these is who is borrowing your money and for how long.

Investing in yourself

needs to be a priority.

The bottom line is that you must have excess earnings to invest. It is only logical that maximizing your earning potential should be a priority, irrespective of your career choice. Some people want to "kill it." For these people, a career is a means to an end. Maximizing earnings is their primary objective. Others choose careers based on a passion. The truly lucky have careers that are both financially and personally rewarding.

Regardless of the path you have chosen, do what it takes to maximize your earning potential. Go above and beyond, whether you are an employee, a professional, or a business owner.

Cash is king only at the flea market.

Cash is king at a flea market or when you are haggling over the price of a used car. Cash as an investment, however, offers safety but little else. By cash investment, I am referring to savings accounts, money market accounts, and short-term certificates of deposit. Keeping cash in these types of accounts feels safe. You know for sure the money is there. That is perfectly acceptable for money you plan to use for an emergency fund, a house down payment, or any other purpose in the near future.

Beyond that, cash is a very poor investment. You are guaranteed to lose money over the long term. Savings accounts and money market funds do not pay much interest. The interest earned rarely if ever keeps up with the inflation rate. Inflation is the general increase in prices. A dollar today will not buy the same amount of goods in the future. If the interest doesn't keep up with inflation, you are losing money in terms of real purchasing power. Then, just to rub a little salt in the wound, you must pay income taxes on the interest earned. Yuck! Add them both together, and you are safely losing money.

A bond is an IOU with a serial number issued by a government, state, city or corporation.

When an ordinary person or small business needs money, they typically go to the bank to request a loan. When governments, states, cities, or large corporations need to borrow money, they issue bonds. Typically, they break the total into $1,000 increments—the face amount—and offer the bonds to the investing public. As an investor, you buy the bond in exchange for receiving annual interest payments. At maturity, you will receive the face amount of the bond. Note that this is different from a bank loan. When you borrow money from a bank, each payment you make consists of principal and interest.

Although stocks represent ownership and bonds represent lending, they have one thing in common: after the issuer brings the bonds to the market and raises the money needed, all future buying and selling of bonds is between investors.

Bonds are subject to default and interest-rate risk.

Default risk is the risk that the issuer will not be able to pay the interest and/or repay the loan. Moody's and Standard & Poor's (S&P) review bond issuers and assign bonds a rating from AAA (or Aaa in the Moody's system), the best, to C, the worst. Bonds with a AAA (or Aaa) rating offer the greatest degree of safety and the lowest interest. Bond ratings below BBB (Moody's Baa) are not considered investment grade and are commonly called high-yield or junk bonds. Junk bonds pay higher interest in exchange for the higher risk of default.

All bonds, regardless of ratings, are subject to interest-rate risk. Interest-rate risk is the potential for bond values to change because of changes in market interest rates. There is an inverse relationship between the change in interest rates and the value of the bond. If rates have fallen, you can sell that bond at a premium. If rates have increased, you will have to sell that bond at a loss. The actual gain or loss depends on how much the interest rates have changed and how much time remains until the bond matures. Interest-rate changes affect long-term bonds to a greater degree than short-term bonds. Because of the greater potential for loss, it is particularly important for investors to consider interest-rate risk when they purchase bonds, especially long-term bonds, when interest rates are low.

Treasury Bonds are issued by

the

US Treasury.

Whenever the government needs money, it issues bonds. These bonds are commonly called treasuries. When investing in treasuries, you are loaning money to the government. Until 2011 treasuries held a rating of AAA. But that year, for the first time in history, treasuries were downgraded from AAA to AA+. However, treasuries are still considered investment grade and continue to be widely regarded as one of the safest forms of investment.

Treasuries are offered in a wide range of maturities. T-bills have a maturity of less than one year. Instead of receiving interest payments, you buy the bill at a discount and receive the full amount at maturity. Treasury notes have maturities ranging from one to ten years. Treasury bonds have maturities from ten to thirty years. Treasury notes and bonds pay interest twice a year equal to the coupon rate times the face value. For example, if a ten-year $1,000 note were offered at 4 percent a year, you would receive $20 every six months for ten years. At the maturity, you would receive the original $1,000.

Municipal bonds are issued by cities, counties, school districts, public utility districts or any other government entity below the state level.

A municipal bond is only as good as the municipal entity that issues it. The bonds are rated based on that entity's perceived ability to repay the loan. Interest income earned on municipal bonds is often exempt from federal income tax and from the income tax of the state in which the bonds are issued.

When you buy a stock, you are buying a piece of a business.

When you own stock, you are a business owner. If you buy shares in Coca-Cola, you own a piece of Coca-Cola. The same thing goes for Facebook, Apple, Google, and all other companies that offer shares. Unlike when you own a private business, you will not be called upon to make key decisions. Questions like "How are we going to handle the union negotiations over health care cost?" or "Should we increase our price to reflect the increase in sugar prices?" will not be up to you. Whew! Day-to-day and long-term strategy is left to the CEO. A board of directors oversees the CEO. Theoretically the board of directors represents the shareholders' best interest.

Except when a stock is first offered for sale (an IPO), all stock trades are made between investors.

Public corporations—companies whose stocks are traded on a stock exchange—start out as privately held businesses. At some point, they need money to grow. One option is to issue stock as an initial public offering (IPO).

Look at Microsoft and Apple. They were started with little more than a dream and some spare parts. The businesses grew rapidly in the late seventies and early eighties. To finance their expansions, both companies went public, meaning they sold ownership to the public in the form of stock. The proceeds from the initial stock sale went back to the companies. Unless a company issues additional stock, the initial sale of stock is the only time the actual company makes money from the stock.

Day-to-day stock trades are between investors. Think about that for a second. One investor is trying to sell while one investor is trying to buy. That means one of them is wrong about the direction of the stock.

There are two ways to make money in stocks: capital appreciation and dividends.

Investors make money in stocks either through capital appreciation or through dividends. Capital appreciation is the primary objective when investing in stocks. The goal is to buy low and sell higher, regardless of how long you plan to hold the stock.

Dividend income is usually a secondary consideration when investing in stocks. When a company earns a profit (and you want to invest only in companies that earn a profit), it has a choice to retain all or part of the profit or to distribute some or all the profit to the shareholders in proportion to the amount of stock that each shareholder owns.

Typically, growing companies retain the profit to reinvest in further expansion or to strengthen their balance sheets. Both actions can help the stock price. If the company has limited expansion opportunity, however, it will pay a dividend.

The dividend yield is calculated as the dividend divided by the current stock price.

When a company declares a dividend, it is a fixed amount per share. In 2014 Coca-Cola declared an annual dividend of $1.22. On March 31, 2014, the stock closed at $36.79 per share. The dividend yield at that price was 3.31 percent ($1.22 divided by $36.79). On November 24, 2014, the stock closed at $44.10 per share. The dividend yield at that price was 2.76 percent ($1.22 divided by $44.10). As you can see, the actual dividend did not change, only the yield. This is very different from an interest-bearing account with a fixed rate. An interest-bearing account offering 2 percent will pay you only 2 percent.

The really cool thing about dividends is that dividend-paying companies typically raise the dividend each year. In 2015 Coca-Cola increased its annual dividend from $1.22 per share to $1.32 per share. That is an 8.2 percent increase in addition to the increased value. If you reinvest the dividend each year, you will further compound your growth.

The not-cool thing about dividends is that unless they are held in a tax-advantaged account, they are taxed annually, even if you reinvest them. Furthermore, dividend-paying stocks do not increase at the same rate as those of companies with increasing profits.

Stock indices measure the total value of a section of the stock market. Widely quoted indices include the Dow, the S&P 500, and the Nasdaq.

The Dow (Dow Jones Industrial Average), the S&P 500, and the Nasdaq are indices of stocks that represent the weighted average value of a section of the stock market.

The Dow comprises thirty large widely held US companies. The companies that make up the index change over the years. Currently the index is made up of American Express, Apple, Boeing, Caterpillar, Chevron, Cisco, Coca-Cola, Du Pont, ExxonMobil, General Electric, Goldman Sachs, The Home Depot, IBM, Intel, Johnson & Johnson, JPMorgan Chase, McDonald's, 3M, Merck, Microsoft, Nike, Pfizer, Procter & Gamble, Travelers, UnitedHealth Group, United Technologies, Verizon, Visa, Walmart, and Walt Disney.

The S&P 500 is a basket of five hundred stocks that represents 80 percent of the total US stock market capitalization; it is widely regarded as the best single gauge of large-market-capitalization US equities. Large market capitalization, also known as large cap or big cap, refers to companies with a market capitalization value of more than $10 billion. If you are interested in looking up the companies that make up the index, go to Yahoo Finance (Finance.Yahoo.com), click on S&P 500, and then click on Components.

The Nasdaq composite, on the other hand, tracks approximately four thousand stocks, all of which are traded on the Nasdaq exchange. The companies tracked by the Nasdaq composite include the world's foremost technology and biotech giants, such as Apple, Google, Microsoft, Oracle, Amazon, Intel, and Amgen.

Over the long term, stocks have provided the best returns.

At the beginning of the book, I talked about Sam, a fictional person used to illustrate the power of compounding. It is an illustration I created in hopes of motivating you to act. That sort of thing got me excited in college.

But reality is more compelling than fiction. Aswath Damodaran is a professor of finance at the Stern School of Business at New York University and the author of several books concerning stock valuation. According to data provided by Damodaran, from 1928 to 2014, the S&P 500 earned an average of 11.53 percent per year, ten-year treasury notes earned 5.25 percent, and T-bills earned 3.53 percent. Translated, $100 invested in the stock market in 1928 would equal $289,995 in 2014, compared to $6,972 for ten-year treasury notes and $1,973 for T-bills.

I can almost hear you saying, "Are kidding me? From 1928 to 2014 is more than seventy years! I will be dead by that time!"

I get it, and I am not suggesting investing for the hell of it. What I am suggesting is that over the long term, stocks provide the best way to create long-term wealth. Let's go back to the first example, in which Sam invested $500 per year until age twenty-four and then $2,500 a year until age thirty. If he invested that money at 11.53 percent, he would have a nest egg of $1,701,000; if he invested it at 5.25 percent, he would have $162,000. That is a $1,500,000 difference! Read it again: a $1,500,000 difference!

Over the short term, stocks have provided the most headaches.

Even though the stock market provides superior long-term investment results, investing in stocks can be a nightmare in the short term. You don't have to look too far back to see this point illustrated. In just three months, from December 2007 to March 2008, the S&P 500 fell by 50 percent and netted a loss of 36.55 percent for the year. (Interestingly enough, ten-year treasury notes earned 20.55 percent that year as result of rapidly falling interest rates.)

I clearly remember March 2008. It was hard to keep calm as I watched my stock portfolio seemingly melt before my eyes. After all, I practice what I preach. This book is based on personal experience. I had spent a lifetime saving and investing, only to see it gone. That was a nightmare, even for me. In my defense, however, the 2008 stock market decline was one for the record books. Yet I hung in there and added to my stocks on the way down and the way up, although admittedly not as much as I should have. In any case, as of 2017, the S&P 500 has more than made up its losses. Nightmare over—for now.

There are two ways to make money in real estate: capital appreciation and rental income.

The popularity of investing in real estate comes and goes. For years, you could not turn on late-night television without hearing about how to buy real estate with no money down, collect rent more than the loan payment, and become a millionaire virtually overnight. Those shows have been replaced with ones about people flipping houses. They make it look so easy to find a fixer-upper at a bargain price, throw on some paint, and install new cabinets and maybe a little tile—voilà, you pocket a hundred grand. I wish it were that easy!

So let's take out the hype and look at real estate as an investment for the average American. On the positive side, real estate offers a diversification from stocks, it offers protection against inflation, and it is something you can touch and visit. In other words, real estate is real.

The cons are that unless you can invest in several properties at one time, you are left with all your proverbial eggs in one basket. That single property can make you or break you. Real estate is also illiquid, meaning that it can be difficult to sell, especially under distress. Another disadvantage is that you must have the ability to continue to commit funds for repairs, maintenance, property taxes, and insurance in the event the property cannot generate income. Finally, if your real estate property is a rental, be ready to take that midnight call when the air conditioning is not working!

Bottom line: buying real estate is real commitment.

If you want to invest in real estate but do not want the hassle or monthly payments, invest in a REIT.

A real estate investment trust (REIT) is a corporation or trust that uses the pooled capital of many investors to purchase and manage income property and/or mortgage loans. REITs are traded on major exchanges just like stocks.

REITs offer several benefits over owning properties. First, they are highly liquid, unlike traditional real estate. Second, REITs enable you to invest in nonresidential properties, such as hotels, malls, and other commercial or industrial properties. Third, there's no minimum investment with REITs.

REITs do not necessarily increase and decrease in value along with the broader stock market. They pay dividends no matter how the shares perform. By law US REITs are required to pay at least 90 percent of taxable income to their shareholders.

On the downside, like stocks, REITs are negatively impacted by economic downturns. Lower occupancy rates mean lower profits. Higher interest rates also translate into lower profit. And because REITs are required to pay out 90 percent of net income, management frequently must use debt to purchase real estate. Finally, the high payout means high taxes, with some being taxed as ordinary income. Yuck!

A mutual fund is not an investment; it is an investment vehicle.

It really bothers me when people say they are invested in mutual funds. It is disturbing because that statement alone tells me that they do not understand what they are invested in and therefore are likely to make some big mistakes.

So, what exactly is a mutual fund, if it's not an investment? In a mutual fund, money is pooled together and invested in stocks, bonds, real estate, cash, or some combination of the above. The ownership of the pooled investments is broken down into shares. Each share represents partial ownership of each investment held within the fund.

A manager is hired to make all the investment decisions. The manager must adhere to the mutual fund's objective. For example, if you invest in a fund focused on small-cap stocks—that is, stocks with a relatively small market capitalization (generally between $300 million and $2 billion)—the manager cannot decide to invest in bonds. The mutual fund is an investment vehicle; the underlying assets are the investment.

An actively managed mutual fund offers professional money management and instant diversification for a small investment but at a high cost.

Selecting individual investments adds another layer of uncertainty in an already-uncertain world. Mutual funds offer instant diversification for an investment as low as $1,000. That $1,000 is spread over thousands of stocks or bonds, something that is impossible to do otherwise. A team of professional money managers is hired to select and manage the money in the mutual fund.

That is the good news. The bad news is that actively managed mutual funds are expensive, perform poorly, and will often increase your tax bill. What? An average actively managed fund charges 1.5 percent of assets. The fund must outperform the market by 1.5 percent just to break even. Unfortunately, nobody has been able to pull that off for very long. That small difference in return will add up.

As a further insult, portfolio managers will buy and sell assets throughout the year to boost returns. During the year, a typical manager will turn over 85 percent of the portfolio. Each buy-and-sell transaction costs money. Each buy-and-sell transaction triggers a tax. It is possible to have a year-end loss of value in an actively traded mutual fund and still have a rather nasty tax bill. I know. I have learned the hard way.

The easiest and most efficient way to invest is through index funds.

It has been well documented that actively managed mutual funds do more harm than good over the long term. (If you are interested in learning more about mutual funds, read Bogle on Mutual Funds: New Perspectives for the Intelligent Investor, by John C. Bogle, founder of the Vanguard Group, an investment company.)

Fortunately, there is a solution, an easy solution: index funds. Index funds seek not to beat the market but simply to match the market. Like their brethren, mutual funds, index funds offer instant diversification. However, they keep expenses and turnover to a minimum. Lower expenses and a lower tax bill mean more money for you.

Another good option is an

Exchange Traded Fund.

Exchange-traded funds (ETFs) are similar in structure to mutual funds, but they are traded like stocks. They provide instant diversification at rock-bottom cost. Many ETFs mimic an index or sector. (A sector ETF invests in a particular industry, such as tech, health care, or utilities.) However, there are a few ETFs that try to beat the market. Beware.

You can choose from hundreds of index funds and ETFs.

My guess is at this point there are more index funds and ETFs to choose from than actual individual stocks that make up the index. Seems crazy, I know. The funds are broken down based on their focus: stocks, bonds, real estate, commodities, and even currencies. The stock funds are further categorized by other factors: United States, international, foreign, large companies, midsized companies, small companies, growth companies, value companies, and sectors (such as tech, health care, and energy). Bonds are also categorized by factors such as investment grade, maturities, and country of origin (United States, international, and foreign), to name a few.

Obviously, the choices can be overwhelming. When you are first starting out and have limited resources to invest, it is best to start with a few total-market funds. For example, you may invest in a total stock market fund, a total bond fund, a US REIT fund, and a foreign fund.

Which is better, an index
mutual fund or an ETF?
A commission-free ETF.

Here are pros and cons to each.

Index Funds: Typically, index funds have high minimum initial investments ranging from $1,000 to as high as $3,000. If you were to break up your investment between four index funds, you would need a minimum of $4,000 before you could make your initial investment. With a budget of $500 per year, it would take you eight years to build a diversified portfolio. That is simply too long.

ETF: The minimum investment in an ETF, on the other hand, is the price per share (assuming no commission). The key, however, is that the ETF must charge no commission fees. A typical $9.99 commission charge would eat up 10 percent of a $100.00 initial investment. So be absolutely sure you are not paying a commission.

Discount brokers, such as TD Ameritrade, offer commission-free ETF trades. As an example, go to the TD Ameritrade website (TDAmeritrade.com) and type commission-free ETF in the search bar. It will give you a list of over one hundred high-quality, commission-free ETFs. You can set up a nice portfolio using VTI (Vanguard Total Stock Market), BND (Vanguard Total Bond ETF), EFV (iShares MSCI—foreign stocks excluding the United States and Canada), and VNQ (Vanguard REIT).

Chapter Eight: Investment Strategies

We simply attempt to be fearful when others are greedy and to be greedy only when others are fearful.

—Warren Buffett

Before you invest in anything, including a good old-fashioned savings account, understand the risk and rewards of each type of investment.

Risk is defined as an unpredictable outcome. If you do not fully understand risk, you will be much more likely to make a rash decision. If unpredictability is expected, you know how to respond. Decisions made from fear and greed are never good decisions. Take the time to understand what you are getting yourself into before investing.

Cash

Pros: Safe, liquid investment.

Cons: No protection against inflation.

Bonds

Pros: Income producer. Greater return than cash.

Cons: Subject to interest-rate risk, especially long-term bonds.

Stocks

Pros: Best long-term performance.

Cons: Unpredictable in the short term.

Real estate

Pros: Added diversification, income, and capital appreciation. Good inflation hedge.

Cons: Access to cash reserves needed for privately held real estate. REITs can mimic stock in terms of volatility and can be poorly managed.

The single biggest risk you face is yourself.

Living too large for your income, waiting until the "right time" to invest, and reacting to market mayhem are the three most financially destructive habits. The American dream seems to require living large: large home, large car, and large lifestyle, all funded with large debt. But too many times the American dream turns into the American nightmare. How about a new dream? How about low fixed costs and large brokerage accounts?

The idea of waiting until the perfect time to invest money is also a problem. Procrastination is born out of fear: fear of making a mistake and fear of losing money. Education will eliminate this fear, or at least reduce it. Don't invest in something you do not understand. Once you understand the investment and risks associated with it, put it on "autopilot." Trust yourself and your decision.

Finally, the most lethal financial mistake is reacting to market mayhem. Look back at the examples in the easy economics section. Big market swings are not a result of some natural disaster. Big market swings happen because people are either buying like crazy or selling like crazy. Markets are not always rational. Don't worry about what happens to your investment balance from day to day. You have time. Stick to the plan. It may not seem cool or exciting, but it sure works.

Bulls and Bears make money;

Pigs and Chickens get served

for dinner.

Bull and bear are terms that refer to the state of the stock market. The phrase bull market means the stock market is up, while the phrase bear market means the stock market is down. When you have a diversified portfolio, you will make money in all markets. One investment zigs and the other zags.

Pigs and chickens, on the other hand, do not make money. A pig is an investor who sees the market climbing and chases that climb, adding more and more money at the height because he doesn't want to miss a penny of gain. Greed sets in and overtakes common sense. It is impossible to precisely time a turn in a market. Pigs get caught adding more at the top and then are forced to sell at the bottom.

Chickens are the exact opposite of pigs. Chickens watch the market fall. When it falls to the point that they simply can't stand losing another penny, they sell. They sit on cash until the market starts to move up again and then buy higher. To make money in stocks, you must buy low and sell high. Pigs and chickens buy high and sell low. Not a good plan.

But the turtle wins the race!

Look at the following example of two choices. Without reading ahead, which of the two would you invest in?

	A	B
Year 1	+25	+10
Year 2	+15	+8
Year 3	−26	+2
Year 4	−5	+3
Year 5	+21	+5
Average return	6.0	4.8

It seems obvious: Investment A. You may be in for a wild ride, but you end up with more money. Right?

Not so fast. You would have more money with investment B. If you invested $10,000, after five years, you would have $12,227 with investment A and $12,506 with investment B. It comes down to compounding. Investment B allows your earnings to earn more earnings, therefore increasing the overall real return. That is the difference between average return and compounded return. Do the math. The turtle—investment B—wins the race. Steady over sexy gets you more money in the bank.

Take advantage of your employer sponsored 401(k) plan.

A 401(k) plan is an employer-sponsored retirement plan that allows you to invest a portion of your earnings before taxes. Furthermore, most employers that offer 401(k) plans also match a portion of your contributions, up to a fixed percentage of your income. They give you money as an incentive to save. It is free money. Take it. All of it.

To illustrate how this works, let's assume your employer offers 25 percent matching, up to 6 percent of your salary. You have a salary of $50,000. Your effective tax rate is 18 percent. (The effective tax rate is the real overall tax rate.) Your contribution would be $3,000 for the year, but your 401(k) balance would be $3,750, before considering the return on your investments. The best part is that your take-home pay would be decreased by only $2,460.

To drive home what a deal this is, I will repeat myself. For only $2,460, you get $3,750! Now I call that Easy Money!

If you qualify, invest in an IRA or a Roth IRA.

Nothing is certain but death and taxes. However, you can postpone the inevitable with an individual retirement account (IRA) or a Roth IRA.

An IRA allows you to deduct your contribution from your taxable income and invest that money. The money will grow, tax deferred, until you retire. That means all your money is working for you to accelerate compounding, as opposed to some of it being taken out to pay taxes. When you retire, your withdrawals will be taxed at your then-current tax rate.

A Roth IRA does not allow you to take a tax deduction for contributions; however, all earnings are tax-free. Yes, I said tax-free. You will never owe an additional penny of tax on your Roth IRA. To qualify, you must have earned some income, but not too much.

I love, love, love a Roth IRA for young people. Here is why. Typically, when you are first starting out, you make very little money. Because your earnings are so low, you owe little to no income tax. I realize money is tight, but if you can take some of that money you have earned, or even money given to you at Christmas or birthdays, and invest it in a Roth IRA, you will be golden—like the golden-egg goose.

First, you will be investing early. Remember Sam at the beginning? Second, you will never owe income taxes on the money on which you paid little or no income tax to begin with. Sweet deal!

Invest in a diversified portfolio of asset types.

The idea behind building a portfolio of different types of investment is to minimize risk while maximizing return. Ideally, when one investment zigs, the other will zag, resulting in a somewhat straight line. You want profit each year because ultimately it is the compounded return that makes money. Think turtle.

Your first decision regarding diversifying is how much to invest in each category. Everyone is different. People have very different goals, risk tolerance, and understanding of investments. As a rule, subtract your age from one hundred to arrive at the amount you should have in stocks versus bonds. This is a conservative amount. That means a twenty-year-old investor's portfolio would be 80 percent stocks and 20 percent bonds.

For a more aggressive allocation, consider 120 minus your age. This allocation would say the same twenty-year-old should have a portfolio of 100 percent stocks. On the other end of the spectrum, if you are very uncomfortable with seeing a loss (albeit a paper loss, because it is not a real loss until you really sell it), a portfolio of 50 percent stocks and 50 percent bonds may be more appropriate and will provide a greater return and less risk than a portfolio of 100 percent bonds.

You can go to the Vanguard website (Vanguard.com) or the iShares website (iShares.com) to build sample ETF portfolios. Even if you do not end up using their ETFs, it is useful to see the allocations they come up with based on how you answer the questions.

Over time, further diversify your investments.

When you are first starting out, you are limited to total-market ETFs, such as VTI (Vanguard Total Stock Market), BND (Vanguard Total Bond ETF), and EFV (iShares MSCI—foreign stocks excluding the United States and Canada).

But as your portfolio grows, you can further diversify within each category. For instance, instead of just a total-market index ETF, you may have a selection of ETFs with dividend-paying stocks, small-cap stocks, large-cap growth stocks, or emerging markets. Just as certain types of investments do better at certain times, certain segments within each type perform better. Sometimes large-company stocks lead the market; other times it is the small growing companies that lead the market. By systematically investing and periodically rebalancing, you will boost your overall return.

For kicks and giggles, use the iShares portfolio builder to construct a hypothetical portfolio using a large initial investment. Notice the difference in recommendations based on the initial investment.

Once you have decided on the right mix of assets, automate the process.

I realize that by this point, I have repeated myself several times regarding automation. It is intentional. I love the idea of automating because it eliminates so many of the problems associated with successful investing. Think of it like that gym you joined and never went to but whose bill you kept paying regularly. OK, you are too smart for that, but so many people are not. The point is, once you get accustomed to having a certain amount diverted from your account, you don't miss it.

More importantly, automation takes the idea of market timing off the table. Market timing is a tempting proposition, especially when you calculate how much money can be made if you get it right. But in reality, market timing looks good only in the rearview mirror. Looking ahead, it is nearly impossible to determine the absolute best time to invest. By committing to an automated monthly investment plan, you know you are buying more during downturns and less during upturns. You are also freeing yourself to focus on what really matters, and that is living your best life.

Once every year or two, sell some of your winners and buy more of your losers to get back to your original plan.

Over time, one part of your portfolio will perform better than expected. Your initial plan may have been to have 80 percent of your portfolio in stocks, but now stocks make up 90 percent of your portfolio. When this occurs, it is smart to rebalance your portfolio. Rebalancing requires that you compare current balances in each category— stocks, bonds, and real estate—to your initial goal. Then adjust.

The adjustments can be done in one of two ways. First, you can sell some your winners, capture that gain, and add to your losers. A perfect time to rebalance would have been in 2008, when the S&P 500 was down 36.55 percent and ten-year treasury notes were up 20.1 percent. You would have captured the gain in treasuries and bought stock when it was depressed. (Note, however, that you will have to pay taxes on the gains if your investments are not in a tax-advantaged account.)

Another way to achieve the same result without tax consequences is to direct your additional savings to the underperforming asset class until it is in line. This will take more time and require that you keep track of the progress. After you have reached your initial plan, revert to your original saving allocation.

Consider roboinvesting.

Roboinvesting is a relatively new but rapidly growing investment platform. Essentially, roboinvesting is a "set it and forget it" model. Sign up, take a series of quizzes to determine your risk tolerance, fund the account, and press **Go**. Some roboinvesting companies have no minimum balances, while others require as little as $500; you can also fund them automatically via your bank account. The companies do all the rest. They pick the ETF for each asset class, they automatically rebalance the account, and once you reach a certain balance, they will perform tax harvesting—all for a very low cost. The two pioneers of roboinvesting are Betterment and Wealthfront.

I really **LOVE** this, especially for beginners. As I have said many times, you are the biggest obstacle you will face. It is one thing to develop a plan; it is another to execute that plan. Roboinvesting makes it easy to execute the plan and stay on course.

Keep accurate records to prevent overpaying taxes.

As you know by now, compound interest is a beautiful thing. But for it to happen, you must reinvest all your dividends and distributions. Unless your investments are in a tax-deferred account, those distributions are taxable every year. Yuck. However, once you have paid tax on that distribution, the IRS considers it an additional investment. Years later, when you go to sell that investment, the gain is not simply the current value minus what you originally bought it for; it is the current value minus your original investment plus all the reinvested distributions over the years. If you do not include the distributions in the cost, you will end up paying taxes twice.

The moral of the story is to keep accurate records. At a minimum, keep a file of your statements. When you sell, hand them over to your accountant. To get an A+++, use a program like Quicken to keep track of your investments. Quicken offers automatic downloads from most brokerages. Easy.

Do not watch your money too closely.

A final yet important strategy is not to watch your money too closely. Spend your time in the beginning becoming comfortable with your initial investment decisions. Strive to continue to learn. Knowledge eliminates fear. But never, under any circumstances, track your money too closely.

It may seem unconventional to put your money on autopilot and then check in only periodically. But there are sound reasons for not watching your money too closely. Common outcomes of closely monitoring your money are either excess optimism or excess fear. When things are going well, you may feel suddenly wealthy. Maybe you skip a few months of investing. Or perhaps you feel as though you are missing out and double up on your investments. On the flip side, when the market is in free fall, it will be hard not to sell to alleviate some of the pain. Trust me: I know.

Be kind to yourself. Allow yourself a quarterly, semiannual, or annual review of your money. Approach it with a level head. Rebalance. Make changes in your plan only in response to changes in your goals, not because of changes in the market, and all will be well.

Chapter Nine: Owning Your Own Business

Real entrepreneurs have what I call the three Ps (and, trust me, none of them stands for permission). Real entrepreneurs have a passion for what they are doing, a problem that needs to be solved, and a purpose that drives them forward.

—Michael Dell

According to Thomas J. Stanley, Author of the Millionaire Next Door, two-thirds of all millionaires are self-employed.

That is an interesting statistic. Especially considering that the US Bureau of Labor Statistics claims that less than 10 percent of the labor force is self-employed. Clearly self-employment can be financially rewarding.

Yet going solo is not without risk. Only 50 percent of start-up businesses make it past the first five years, and only 35 percent past the first ten years. It is that risk-reward thing all over again: the greater the risk, the greater the potential return.

You must have the proper mental attitude.

Before you go dashing off to flip over the OPEN sign, do a little soul searching. Not everyone is cut out to be self-employed. It takes a certain personality. I am not sure I can provide an adequate description of entrepreneurs, because their personalities are as diverse as the businesses they run. However, there are some key common attitudes.

Passion. Passion for what you are doing, for building a business, or for making money is the fuel needed to get through the rough times.

Confidence. If you don't believe in yourself, how do you expect others to?

Perseverance. Perseverance is the ability to get up after falling. Expect to fall. The question is, how many times will you get back up?

Ability to learn from setbacks. This goes hand in hand with perseverance. It is one thing to get back up when knocked down but another to figure out how to prevent a repeat performance.

Adaptability. As a business owner, you are making the rules. What worked at the beginning may no longer work as you grow. Things change, and so must you to remain relevant and viable.

Different view of risk. For most people, risk is defined as uncertainty about the future. In fact, I used this very definition in the previous section on investment. But business owners see working for someone else as the greater risk. They do not trust their futures in the hands of another. They also view the risk of doing nothing as greater than that of committing to a well-thought-out plan.

Do you see yourself as self-employed or as an entrepreneur?

On the surface, being self-employed and being an entrepreneur appear to be the same. Self-employment means you work for yourself. You are the heart of the business. The success or failure of the business, regardless of the number of employees, is dependent on you. Without you, the business crumbles. Entrepreneurs, on the other hand, are business builders. The objective is for the business to survive without the continued presence of the founder.

Consider Amanda George and Alli Webb. Both are hugely successful hair stylists, but they could not be more different in terms of their business models. George has perfected her talent. She is an internationally acclaimed celebrity hair stylist and has received national acclaim in the world's leading fashion publications, including Allure, Harper's Bazaar, Cosmopolitan, and Vogue. She is known for catering to an exclusive clientele. George is the business.

In contrast, Alli Webb, the founder of Dry Bar Salons, perfected a process, the forty-minute blowout. The experience, down to style options, decor, and even playlist, is consistent regardless of location or stylist. The process is the business.

Do what you know.

Not having experience is commonly listed as the number-one reason for business failure. Do what you know. That may seem obvious. But what do you really know?

Assume you know how to make the best brick-oven pizza. Everyone is always raving about it. You are confident that you have something special and different to offer. But does that mean you also know how to run a successful pizzeria? On the surface, it may seem as if having a superior pizza would be enough. But there is so much more to running a successful restaurant than the food. Location, pricing, supplier relationships, kitchen staff, front-of-house staff, overall atmosphere, and decor are just a few of the other important elements. Just because you know how to make a great pizza does not mean you know how to run a great restaurant.

If you are unsure, get some on-the-job training. You will see up close and personal what works and what doesn't. That is why doctors must finish residency programs before becoming licensed. Contractors are also required to have several years' real-life experience before becoming licensed. Experience matters.

An alternate strategy is to consider a franchise. Franchise companies have established themselves within their markets, fended off competitive elements, honed their systems and processes, learned from mistakes, made the necessary course corrections, formed supplier relationships, and attracted loyal customers. They have beaten the odds, and now they want to impart everything they've learned to you—for a price.

Know your strengths and weaknesses.

Perfection is an illusion. It is destructive to think that you can be all things to all people. Instead, find what you do best and outsource the rest. (Hey, that rhymes!) Not good at numbers? Hire an accountant. Not good at website design? Hire a designer. You get the idea.

Alli Webb, founder of Dry Bar, had a vision for future hair salons that focused exclusively on blowouts. She knew the process, the customer, and the potential. To make her vision a reality, she enlisted the aid of her brother, Michael London, a branding and marketing professional who had worked on behalf of Yahoo, Starwood Hotels, and the Plaza Hotel, to name a few. Although London did not initially share Webb's vision, together they filled each other's gaps and created an extraordinarily successful company.

Sophia Amoruso, the founder of Nasty Gal, worked hard to build her brand from a small eBay storefront to the multimillion-dollar company that it is today. She was the creative force behind the brand. She chose the clothes and styled the shoots. As the business expanded, so did her role as a leader and manager.

In early 2015, however, Amoruso relinquished control of the company she had created and moved back to creative brand building. She recognized that management was not her forte and that the company would be better served with her as the brand developer. Smart.

Regardless of the size of the company, it is smart to focus your time and abilities on the things you do best and get help with the rest.

Know the numbers.

Before you put out the OPEN sign, you need to know the numbers. Ask yourself these questions: What are my fixed costs? What are my variable costs? What needs to happen to break even? Can this location support that level of business?

These are important questions. Most start-ups, if not all, do not make a profit out of the gate. However, you need to be sure that there is at least a potential for profit based on your cost structure.

Imagine opening a wood-fired artisan pizzeria featuring all fresh, organic ingredients. It costs $3.00 to make each pizza. You plan to offer the pizza at $12.50 per pie. That is a gross margin of $9.50. So far, so good. But you can't stop there. You also must consider labor, rent, insurance, electricity, and other expenses. When you add up all the fixed costs, you are looking at a minimum of $5,000.00 per month. Given that, you would need to sell a minimum of 526 pizzas a month to break even.

Ask yourself, based on other businesses in the area and the demographics, whether the location selected can support that level of sales volume. If not, what can you do to increase the potential for profit? Find a better location? Increase the price? Offer high-margin add-ons? Knowing the numbers is the key to making good decisions.

But knowing the numbers is not something you do just at the beginning; it is an ongoing process. The numbers provide the road map for your business. Only with this road map will you be confident that you are headed in the right direction. Number don't lie.

Keep good records.

I am a CPA, and even I don't like to do bookkeeping. Yet it is vital to the health of your business. Start with the basics: employees. As an employer, you are responsible for withholding, paying, and recording payroll taxes. Mess this up, and the IRS gets difficult. It does not play around when it comes to payroll taxes, because failing to pay these taxes properly is treated as stealing from your employees and from the IRS itself.

Then comes billing. Overbilling and under billing customers are equally bad. Overbilling a costumer creates ill will. Under billing hurts your profitability.

True story: As part of an insurance claim, we hired a contractor to replace our roof, which had been damaged by a hailstorm. The insurance company withheld the final payment until the work was completed and documented. After eighteen months, the roofing contractor still had not completed the paperwork needed to collect the final payment. Although the company did good work on the roof, it was a poorly run business.

Good record keeping goes beyond basic payroll, billing, and payments. As mentioned earlier, the numbers provide the basis for all financial decisions. Bad numbers mean bad decisions. Plenty of programs are available to help with record keeping, even if you are not an accountant. QuickBooks is probably the most popular. If you are completely unsure where to start, hire a CPA for a few hours to get you set up. The CPA can also do the quarterly reporting on your behalf.

Protect what is yours.

Going into business is an exciting time. Only optimists even dare to take on the process. But it is smart to think of the things that can go wrong before anything does go wrong.

Regardless of the type of business you own, it is always good to have some form of liability insurance. It can be a professional errors-and-omissions policy, a personal-umbrella policy, or a business-liability policy. Because these policies have so many variables, it is best to talk to a broker who specializes in your industry.

In addition, be aware of state laws concerning personal assets. In the event the business fails—of course it won't, but just in case—are your assets protected? You need to know whether your personal home is at risk. And what about retirement accounts and IRAs? Trust funds? Spouse assets? Know your state laws and plan accordingly.

Don't underestimate your

digital presence.

When you are a business owner, your digital presence takes on a whole new meaning. When you were in college, you could post all those drunk-at-the-bar pictures, and all you had to worry about was whether your parents would see them. You might have gotten a phone call or lecture, but that was the extent of the damage.

Not so when you own a business. Your digital presence is the face of the business. Even if you have a traditional brick-and-mortar storefront, you can expect people to Google your business. They will look at your website, get directions, and look at reviews. If you have a sloppy website, incomplete information, and bad reviews, you are going to lose business. Furthermore, if your business is based on your personal reputation or professional skills, those college postings may come back to haunt you.

Make it a priority to monitor your digital footprint. Respond to bad reviews in a respectful manner, and offer to rectify the situation if you made an error or did not deliver quality customer service. If, on the other hand, you are being harassed, there are services that will help you legally remove unjust malicious reviews.

Remove and un tag yourself from any photos that would reflect badly on you or your business. And most importantly, request that your satisfied customers give you a positive review on Google, Yelp, or some similar forum. An abundance of good reviews will outweigh a few negative ones.

Chapter Ten: Home Sweet Home

There's no place like home.

—Dorothy Gale

It is not always a good idea

to own a home.

Home ownership is the American dream. White picket fences and apple pie—I get it. I believe in it. I own my home. But it is not always a smart idea to buy a home.

If you are unsure about your future, do not buy a home. Buying and selling a house is very expensive. Under normal circumstances, it takes five years just to break on the transaction costs alone. So, if your plan doesn't extend beyond a year or two, forgo the home.

Next, if you choose to live in an expensive area, such as New York City or San Francisco, be very careful about what, if anything, you buy. In 2009, the median home prices in those areas were almost seven times higher than the median income. In the rest of the country, the median home price hovers between two and three times the median income. What does that mean for your checkbook? That means that you must earn much more than the median income and allocate a higher percentage of your income toward housing costs. Carefully consider your personal long-term goals. If you love the city and cannot imagine living anywhere else, know that you will have to work longer and harder to overcome the extra burden of the high housing cost. Ask yourself whether it is worth it.

Finally, if you are looking at an area where property values have jumped suddenly, do a little digging. Were properties undervalued for many years and are now getting in line with the rest of the country, or are you in an overheated local market poised for a fall? These are tough questions that require thorough research.

Is your home an investment?

If you are like most people, the biggest real estate purchases you will make is your home. But is that an investment? In one sense it is, because an investment is anything to which you devote money and time with the hope of more money in the future. In that respect, your home is an investment, because its value will most likely increase over time.

But the question is, how do you get money out of your house? You can sell it, but then you must buy another home. This works well if you are moving from a high-priced area like New York to a low-cost area like Tennessee. You could buy a new home and pocket some cash. Another option for getting cash out of your house is through a reverse mortgage, in which you give up equity in your home in exchange for a monthly check.

Personally, I prefer to look at home ownership as a hedge against inflation, and a pretty good one at that. By owning a home, you are locking in tomorrow's expenses today. Just ask your parents or grandparents how much they paid for their first home. You will be utterly amazed. It's that compound interest thing again. The goal is—or at least it used to be—to purchase a home and pay it off over a number of years, thereby eliminating a huge portion of your living expenses. Freedom is to be free from obligations.

Get prequalified before shopping for a home.

Before shopping for a new home, get prequalified or preapproved for a loan. You will need to get all your financial documents in order: tax returns, loan statements, and other related items. Based on the information you provide; a lender will prequalify you for a certain amount. Here is where that great FICO score will pay off. The lower the interest rate, the more home you can afford.

This process takes all the guesswork out of knowing how much to spend on a home. Nothing is worse than finding the home of your dreams and discovering that you can't get the financing. As a bonus, many sellers prefer prequalified buyers so that they don't get stuck taking their homes off the market only to find out the buyers can't go through with the purchase.

Once you have been preapproved, make sure that you are comfortable with all the costs of homeownership. As a homeowner, you are responsible for the property taxes, insurance, HOA fees, repairs, and maintenance. If you are looking at older homes, you will need to be prepared to make repairs, big and small.

Just because a mortgage broker says "yes" doesn't mean you should.

So how much should you borrow? Technically, your total debt payments cannot exceed 35 percent of your gross income. Total debt payments include your mortgage, auto loans, and any other debt. The question is, should you borrow up to 35 percent of your gross income? If you want to work until age seventy and be a slave to your money, sure, go ahead and borrow that much. If your debt is 35 percent of your gross income, your income tax rate is 20 percent, and the FICA tax is 7.65 percent, you are left with only 37 percent of your income to pay for everything else: food, electricity, water, insurance, gas, and clothing. And that doesn't even begin to consider saving.

Not a good plan. A better plan is to limit your housing cost to 25–30 percent of your net income. That means that a week's net take-home earnings will cover your mortgage. Keeping your overheard low will give you freedom that few will enjoy. While others around you will be stretched to the very end, having to watch every penny, you will have peace of mind and be able to afford to build a life you want instead of being tied to an expensive mortgage.

Fixed rate or an adjustable rate mortgage?

Easy.

If interest rates are close to or below long-term averages, get a fixed-rate loan.

If interest rates are significantly above the long-term average, get an adjustable rate mortgage (ARM). Look for a five-year or seven-year ARM with a rate at least 1.5 percent lower than the fixed rate.

When shopping for a mortgage, look at the online mortgage websites. I have personally used LendingTree (LendingTree.com) with great success. Once you have narrowed your search, request a truth-in-lending estimate. Not all mortgage companies are the same. Some add little surprises on the closing statements.

If you are comparing ARMs, check the initial interest rate, how quickly and by how much a rate can change, and the maximum rate. Don't be lured in by a super-low teaser rate that increases quickly or by an interest-only loan. They are sneaky ways to get people into a mountain of trouble. If you cannot afford the loan at the standard rate, you cannot afford the house. It is that simple.

Do your homework before buying a home.

Buying a home is an exciting time, a new chapter in your life, full of possibilities and hope. It is easy to get caught up in the moment. Before you make any real decisions, do your homework. First, consider where exactly you want to live and why. Consider commutes to work, future building that might take place in the area, and school systems. Long commutes are expensive and get old quickly. Future building will impact the value of your home. If the home is in a fully developed area, the values should be stable. If, however, you select a new and growing area, realize that the value of your home can be held down by the ever-growing supply of new homes. And don't forget the schools. Even if you do not have children, a future buyer may. Good schools are on the top of the list for many buyers.

Once you have narrowed your search to specific homes, do a little research on your own. Look for recent sales in the neighborhood you are considering. Calculate the sales price per square foot. Throw out the highest and lowest. Look at the average sales price per square foot and compare that to the property you are considering. Unless you are looking in an area with tract homes, you will need to allow for differences between the homes—things like swimming pools, lot size, and location.

As a final point, I want to emphasis the word homework. Do this on your own. Do not rely on the real estate agent. Some agents are good and some are bad, but all are paid based on the cost of the home you buy. Do your own homework—no cheating.

To get a great bargain, look beyond the ugly.

Pretty homes sell for more money. It is a fact. If you have gone to a new housing development, you will see that the model homes are decked out. The builders bring in a team of decorators to make the home look irresistible. Homeowners will pay for staging companies to stage their properties. That is because a well-decorated home gets a higher price. It is hard for many people to see beyond the current homeowner's designs. It may take some practice, but if you can learn to look at the bones of the house and not the decor, you can potentially save thousands. It is amazing what a fresh coat of paint can do!

Always get an inspection.

Unless you are purchasing a new home with a warranty, get an inspection from a qualified home inspector. This is not the place to save money. Make your offer subject to inspection. If nothing is found during the inspection, proceed with the purchase. If something significant is discovered, you can either withdraw your offer or renegotiate the contract.

Your home is not a piggy bank.

I love piggy banks. They are so cute. I have several. Regardless of how cute your home is; however, it is not a piggy bank. As you build equity in your home through price appreciation and by paying off your original mortgage, don't be tempted to use that equity to pay for more stuff.

Just before the recent real estate collapse, many people were lured into borrowing against the equity they had built in their homes. Banks offered unbelievable deals and used creative marketing to get people hooked. They showed them how much their houses had appreciated and how they could use that equity to buy fun stuff, such as exotic vacations, new cars, and pools. It was all very tempting. Many homeowners succumbed to temptation and took out sizable loans, only to watch their equity vanish.

Even though the recent real estate bubble was a rare occurrence fueled by low interest rates, lax lending practices, and high demand, resulting in volatile real estate valuations, it still does not make sense to rob your home of your equity. The beautiful thing is that if you keep your mortgage cost down, you will have enough money to pay cash for the things you really want. Now that makes sense (and cents, too)!

Chapter Eleven:

Protecting What Is Yours

Expect the best. Prepare for the worst. Capitalize on what comes.

—Zig Ziglar

Insurance is hardship avoidance that cannot be avoided.

Insurance is preparing for bad things in advance. You are required by law to carry auto and health insurance. If you own a home, your lender will require that you carry insurance on it. Other types of insurance, such as disability, life, and umbrella insurance, are discretionary. The amounts and types of insurance you need depend on your current circumstances. In a nutshell, the more you earn and the more stuff you have, the more insurance you will need.

Unless you have an old car and very little money, carry more auto insurance than the state-required minimums.

States require you to carry a minimum level of insurance, although the actual amount required varies from state to state.

Auto insurance has four components: liability, collision/comprehensive, personal injury protection (PIP), and uninsured motorist.

Liability insurance pays for damage you cause. It pays for the other person's medical bills, lost wages, and property damage. Liability coverage is usually stated in a format similar to 50/100/10. That means your insurance will cover a maximum of $50,000 for bodily injuries per person, $100,000 per accident, and $10,000 in property damage. If you cause an accident that results in damages more than your insurance limits, you will need to come up with the difference. If you have assets to protect or wages that could be garnished, keep your limits at a minimum of 100/300/50.

Collision and comprehensive insurance covers damage done to your car. The state does not require that you cover damage to your car, but a finance company will. Consider the age and value of the car when determining whether to carry collision coverage. The older the car, the less likely it makes sense to carry collision.

PIP insurance covers your medical expenses in the event of an accident. If you have good medical and disability insurance, this is redundant.

Uninsured/underinsured motorist insurance pays for your medical bills, pain and suffering, and lost wages if an uninsured driver strikes your car or if you're the victim of a hit-and-run.

Shop for auto insurance each year.

I don't know why, but there can be huge price differences between auto insurance carriers. I have seen differences more than 100 percent between large well-known carriers. The process of comparing doesn't take very long, and you can save big. Easy Money.

You can purchase health insurance individually or through your employer.

Despite the ever-changing laws surrounding health insurance, it is important that you have a plan in place. If you do not have an employer based plan, contact an independent health insurance broker. A good broker will be able to advise you on the current laws and provide options available that fit your needs and budget.

In most cases, your group health insurance will be the best option, because the insurance carriers, and in certain cases the government, require the employer to contribute toward the cost of the insurance. In addition, your portion of the premium contributions is likely to be pretax, which means the money is taken out of your paycheck before taxes are calculated. Conversely, if you choose to purchase health insurance directly rather than through your employer, you will have to pay 100 percent of the premium and lose the tax advantage.

Let's look at the numbers. If the monthly premium for individual coverage is $325, your employer contributes 50 percent, and your marginal income tax rate is 20 percent, your net monthly cost will be $117. That is a much better deal.

You need life insurance only if someone would suffer financially if you were to die.

Life insurance is something you grow into and out of throughout your life. When you first start out as a single person taking on the world, you have no need for life insurance. Many people might be sad if you were to die, but nobody would be hurt financially.

Then come the spouse and the kids. The loss of a spouse/parent is devastating to a family. That loss is compounded when money suddenly becomes scarce. Even parents who stay home with the children should be covered by life insurance. Stay-at-home parents do not provide an income, but they provide a service that will cost money to replace.

Later, over time, as you accumulate money and your obligations decrease, your need for life insurance also decreases.

The easiest and most cost-effective way to get life insurance is to purchase a level-term insurance policy. What does that mean? Level term is life insurance for a term of five, ten, fifteen, or twenty years. You pick. The premium stays the same over the term. It can be canceled without penalty and is far cheaper than permanent life insurance. On average, you will be OK with a policy that covers ten times your salary. As added protection, you can add the amount of outstanding debt, such as mortgages or home loans.

As with health insurance, an independent agent who represents many carriers is your best option. Your insurance premium is the same whether you work with an agent or go direct. Good agents are like personal shoppers: they will seek out the best deals and pass them on to you.

Chapter Twelve:

One More Thing…

Our greatest weakness lies in giving up. The most certain way to succeed is always to try one more time.

—Thomas A. Edison

If you are in a committed relationship, have the money talk.

It is an unfortunate fact, but money affects all aspects of your life. Where you live, the car you drive, the places you go, and even the friends you have are, to some degree, affected by money. Money also has a big impact on personal relationships. If you are in a committed relationship that you expect will lead to marriage, or if you are married already, you need to have the "money talk."

Honesty is key. You need to discuss your money styles. Are you a spender or a saver? Are you conservative or a risk taker? What are your feelings about debt? What are your long-term financial goals? If you plan to have children, do you plan for a parent to stay at home or for both to work outside the home? What kind of house do you want? How will you pay for the house? How much savings and/or debt do you already have?

It is hard to believe, but many people who will discuss other very personal subjects are reluctant to talk openly about money. To make a relationship work, the people involved must be financially as well as emotionally compatible. Create a plan together. You are a team. As a team, you must develop a plan that supports all team members.

If things go wrong along the way, don't blast your partner or hold him or her financially hostage. Review the plan and find out why it didn't work. Adjust and come up with a new winning strategy. Learn to work together to build a financially strong relationship as well as an emotionally strong one, and you will be way ahead of the pack.

Never lend money to family or friends unless you are prepared to never see it again.

If you want to see a relationship crumble, lend money to a friend or relative. Here is what happens. You, as a responsible adult, not spending all you make but instead living within your means, have set aside some money. Your friend gets into a financial bind and needs some help. You, being the good friend that you are, lend your friend some money.

A few weeks go by, and you see your friend's picture on Instagram having the time of her life. Or you go out to dinner, and she orders a cocktail and an appetizer while you stick to the special. Or maybe she shows up with a brand-new pair of shoes. You get the idea. At some point that little voice in your head will be saying, "Wait a minute. Where is my money?" A few more weeks go by, and that little voice turns into full-blown resentment. I have seen it over and over again.

Here is the thing: to save your sanity and relationship, if you lend money to a friend or relative, consider it a gift. You do not need to tell him or her you are considering it a gift, because if you do, you will certainly never see it again. Just within your own mind, think of it as a gift. Then, when and if you are repaid, you have received a gift in turn.

Expect setbacks.

My mom once said to me, "You can't taste the sweet without the sour." Although she didn't clarify what she meant by that statement, I assume she meant that only through our struggles and setbacks do we truly enjoy the triumphs. Expect setbacks in all areas of your life. It's through these setbacks that you learn and grow as a person.

When it comes to investing, setbacks are unavoidable. Stock markets routinely experience both bull and bear markets. A bear market is a decrease in stock prices of 20 percent or more lasting at least sixty days. The US stock market has risen more than it has declined since 1929, but in that same period, the market has experienced twenty-five bear markets, an average of one every 3.4 years, each lasting an average of ten months. Having experienced several bear markets, I can tell you this: you feel a bear market more than a bull market. When your $100,000 stock portfolio goes to $80,000, you feel it more intensely than when your stock portfolio goes from $100,000 to $120,000.

It might help to think of bear markets as winter. You hate it, but it must come. Best to be prepared and look forward to spring. By contrast, imagine living in a world of perpetual spring and then being hit by a snowstorm. It would seem like the end of the world. Knowing what to expect makes all the difference. Expect setbacks in your investments, your career, and your life. They are part of the journey.

Keep learning.

If you have gotten to this page in the book, you are a rare bird indeed. Congratulations! You have shown commitment to building a better life. But don't let it stop here. Continue to learn and grow. It is through this growth that you will gain confidence in your decisions and ultimately gain control over your financial life. You can build a life of your choosing instead of merely reacting or relying on others.

This book is about money and

wealth accumulation,

life is not.

If you are not already familiar with the 1843 Charles Dickens classic A Christmas Carol, check it out. The story is centered on Ebenezer Scrooge, a man who has devoted his life to accumulating wealth. In that endeavor he has succeeded, but at what cost? He is alone, unhappy, and bitter.

Three ghosts visit and show him "what was, what is, and what will be." In one night, he relives the loss of his fiancée; witnesses the suffering that Bob Cratchit, his assistant, must endure; and faces the fact that his death will not be mourned. The moral of the story is that money cannot buy happiness.

If you dig a little deeper into the story, however, you find that money can buy a certain level of happiness. After the last ghost departs, Ebenezer Scrooge is transformed. He provides life-saving medical care for Tiny Tim, Bob Cratchit's sickly son, bringing untold joy and happiness to the Cratchit family.

Although Bob Cratchit appears to be happy even though he's poor, in reality, not having enough money to meet basic needs is extremely stressful. Living long term in a stressful situation undermines your health and relationships. The point of this entire book is to illustrate that you do not need to live the life of either Ebenezer Scrooge or Bob Cratchit. It is true that wealth accumulation alone will not bring happiness. Life is about relationships and experiences. However, by applying the concepts in this book, you can create a full life and have a full bank account.

All you really need to know…

This book has over twenty-three thousand words but can really be boiled down to this short list:

1. Start now.

2. Save and invest a minimum of 10 percent of gross earnings. I don't care what you do with the rest.

3. Automate the process. Eliminate temptation. You can't spend it if you can't see it.

4. Consider roboinvesting. Wealthfront and Betterment are two good choices.

5. Practice gratitude. It makes you a happier person.

6. Continue to learn about money and finances.

7.Stay out of unessential debt.

8.Finally, remember that material things do not bring happiness. Invest in relationships and experiences, because the truly best things in life are free.

Live well and prosper!